WOOL CARDER BEE

(COLLECTS FUZZY FIBERS FROM PLANTS TO LINE ITS NEST!)

EUROPEAN HONEYBEE

(WORLD'S MOST COMMON HONEYBEE!)

CELLOPHANE BEE

(LINES UNDERGROUND NEST WITH A SECRETION THAT DRIES TO LOOK LIKE CELLOPHANE!)

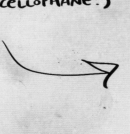

COMMON BUMBLEBEE

(IS A MASTER OF TOMATO POLLINATION!)

GIVE Bees A CHANCE

WORDS & PICTURES by bethany bARTon

VIKING

SURE YOU DO!

DIDN'T I TELL YOU THERE ARE ABOUT 25,000 DIFFERENT KINDS OF BEES TO LOVE?

EUROPEAN HONEYBEE

LEAF-CUTTER BEE

EASTERN CARPENTER BEE

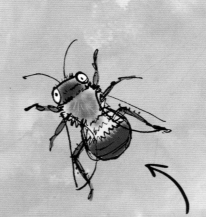

SOUTHEASTERN BLUEBERRY BEE

SQUASH BEE

MINING BEE

AND THEN I TOLD YOU ALL ABOUT the THREE TYPES OF HONEYBEES!

QUEENS

LARGE, FERTILE FEMALE
JOB: MAKE ALL OF THE BABY BEES

JUST 1 PER HIVE

DRONES

300-500 PER HIVE

LARGE MALES WITH NO STINGER
JOB: FIND A QUEEN TO MATE WITH

AND WORKERS

SMALL, STERILE FEMALES WITH STINGERS
JOB: EVERYTHING ELSE!

GATHER NECTAR, POLLEN, & WATER, MAKE HONEY, FEED BABY BEES (LARVAE), BUILD & PROTECT THE HIVE, MAKE ROYAL JELLY TO FEED THE QUEEN... AND MORE!!

30,000-80,000 PER HIVE

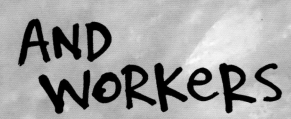

MAYBE I JUST NEED TO REMIND YOU HOW WEIRD AND COOL A HONEYBEE'S ANATOMY IS?

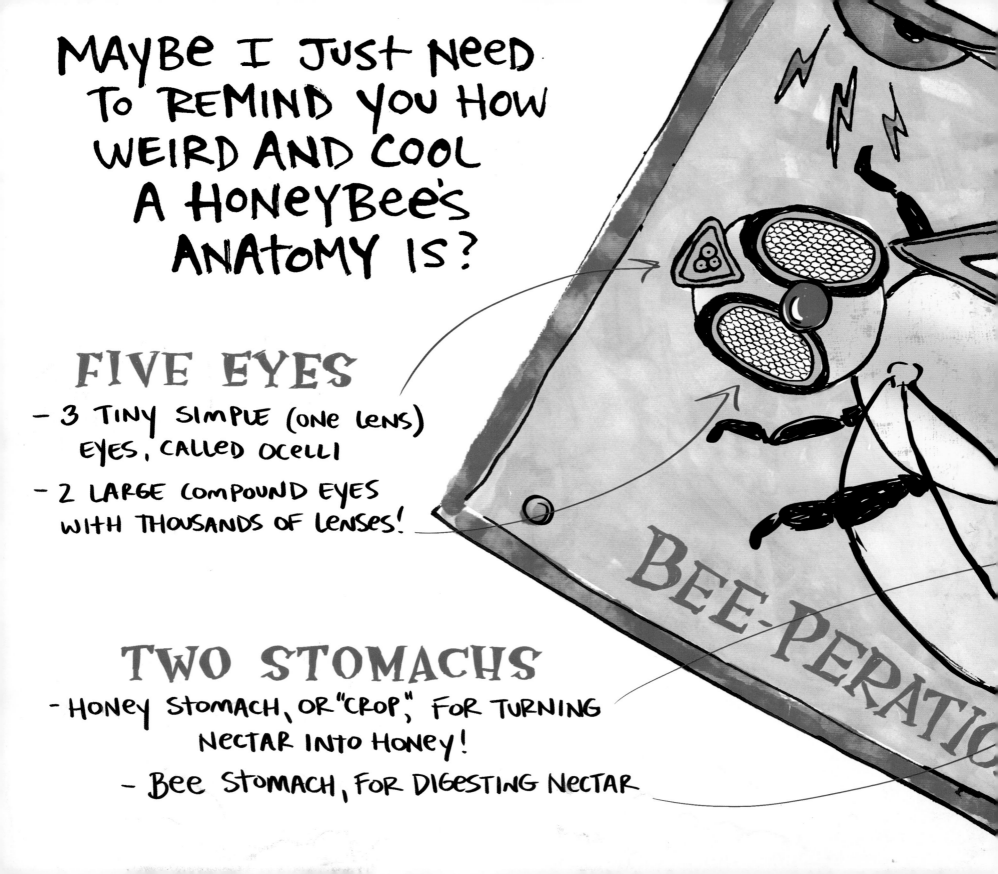

FIVE EYES

- 3 TINY SIMPLE (ONE LENS) EYES, CALLED OCELLI
- 2 LARGE COMPOUND EYES WITH THOUSANDS OF LENSES!

TWO STOMACHS

- HONEY STOMACH, OR "CROP", FOR TURNING NECTAR INTO HONEY!
- BEE STOMACH, FOR DIGESTING NECTAR

BEE-PERATIO

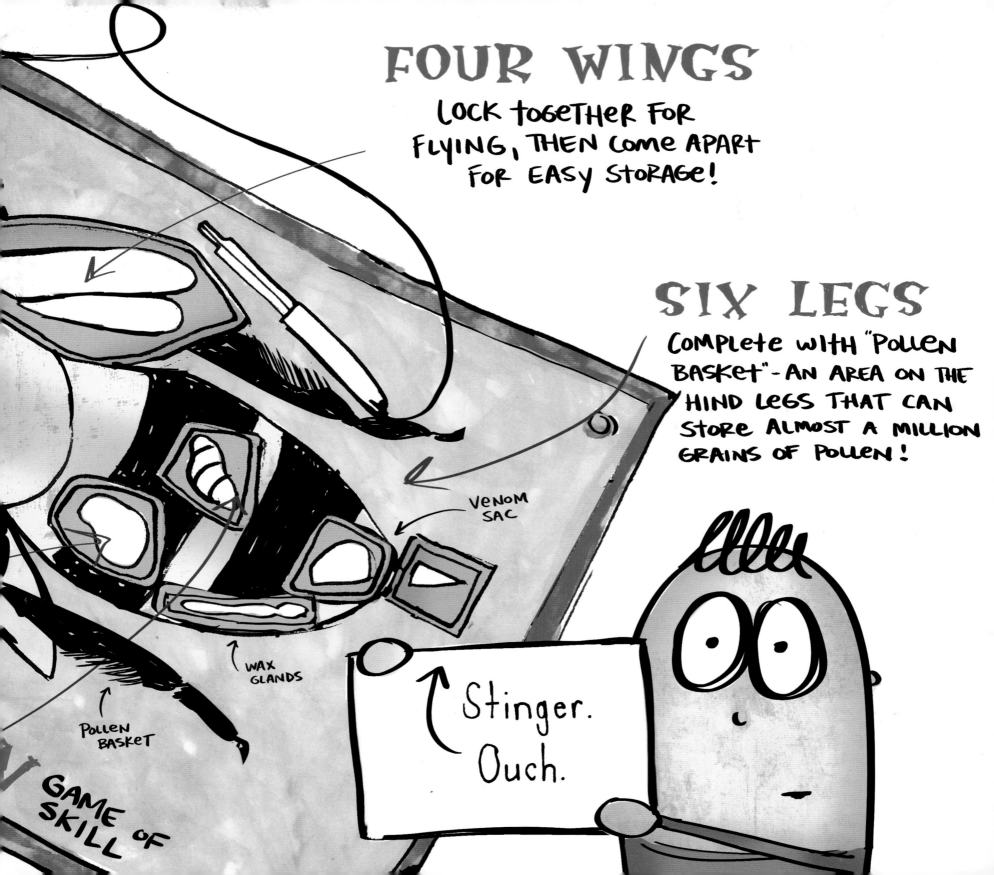

MAYBE YOU JUST NEED SOME TIME TO GET TO KNOW THEM? HOW ABOUT MILLIONS OF YEARS!

YOU KNOW, BEES LIVED WITH DINOSAURS.

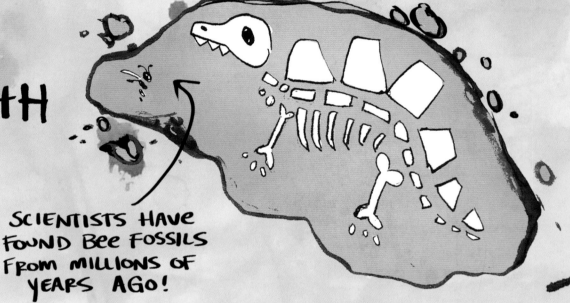

SCIENTISTS HAVE FOUND BEE FOSSILS FROM MILLIONS OF YEARS AGO!

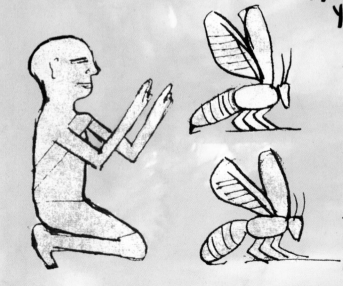

AND EVEN ANCIENT EGYPTIANS KEPT BEES.

HIEROGLYPHIC SYMBOL FOR BEE

IN FACT, HONEY FROM BEES WAS FOUND IN EGYPTIAN TOMBS...

Ooh! Honey!

AND IT WAS STILL EDIBLE!

PERFECT! MAYBE YOU JUST NEED SOME HONEY!

BEES MAKE HONEY!

Why are you telling me all this stuff?

SO YOU'LL GIVE BEES A CHANCE!

ONCE YOU LEARN HOW GREAT THEY ARE, YOU'RE BOUND TO FALL IN LOVE WITH THEM!

CHECK OUT HOW HONEY IS MADE!

A BEE GATHERS NECTAR FROM FLOWERS

NECTAR GOES INTO A SPECIAL HONEY STOMACH CALLED A "CROP"

X-RAY VISION

WHO EACH BREAK DOWN THE NECTAR IN THEIR CROPS UNTIL IT BECOMES HONEY

THEN THE HONEY GETS BARFED INTO A HONEYCOMB CELL

AND FANNED BY THE WINGS OF BEES TO EVAPORATE MOISTURE

CONTENTS OF THE CROP ARE SPIT UP INTO A NEW BEE'S MOUTH

THE NEW BEE BREAKS DOWN THE SUGARS OF THE NECTAR WITHIN HER OWN CROP.

THIS PROCESSED NECTAR IS PASSED ALONG TO SEVERAL MORE BEES

LASTLY, IT'S SEALED WITH BEESWAX TO KEEP IT SAFE (UNTIL IT'S EATEN)

...did you say barf?

JUST ONE POUND OF HONEY TAKES TWO MILLION FLOWERS AND THOUSANDS OF BEES to CREATE...

IT LOOKS LIKE I HAVEN'T CONVINCED YOU JUST YET...

Nope! Because they're all gonna sting me!

OH. WELL, BEES <u>DO</u> STING <u>SOMETIMES</u>... BUT NOT BECAUSE THEY'RE MEAN!

STINGER STORIES

Bees ONLY STING to DEFEND THEMSELVES

YOU LOOK DELICIOUS!

BACK OFF!

OR to AVOID GETTING SQUISHED

OR SMASHED

IN FACT, MANY BEES LOSE THEIR STINGER AFTER ATTACKING

WHICH IS SORT of LIKE YOUR HAND DISAPPEARING IF YOU PINCH YOUR SISTER!

You know, I love honey... but I'd be willing to give it up forever to never see a bee again.

BUT GIVING UP BEES MEANS GIVING UP SO MUCH MORE THAN JUST HONEY!

SOME SCIENTISTS SAY BEES ARE RESPONSIBLE FOR A THIRD OF ALL THE FRUITS AND VEGETABLES WE EAT!

HONEY

BEES HAVE A BIG IMPACT ON THE FOOD CHAIN.

You See, IN ORDER FOR PLANTS to GROW FRUITS AND VEGETABLES. THEY NEED the RIGHT INGREDIENTS.

SUN

WATER

POLLEN

A MAJOR INGREDIENT THEY NEED IS POLLEN.

BUT SINCE FLOWERS CAN'T MOVE, THEY CAN'T ALWAYS GET POLLEN FROM EACH OTHER.

I WANT to MAKE A STRAWBERRY... THROW ME SOME POLLEN!

I DON'T HAVE ARMS.

THAT'S WHERE BEES FLY IN...

A BEE'S FUZZY BODY CATCHES POLLEN FROM FLOWERS.

POLLEN FALLS INTO THE NEXT FLOWER THE BEE VISITS.

THEY ACT AS A POLLEN DELIVERY SERVICE, HELPING GIVE FLOWERS THE INGREDIENTS THEY NEED.

A SINGLE BEE CAN VISIT OVER 1,000 FLOWERS A DAY, MAKING BEE POLLINATION POWERS UNPARALLELED!

WHICH MEANS WITHOUT BEES, THERE'D BE A LOT LESS YUMMY STUFF TO EAT.

MILK

HAVE YOU SEEN THIS POLLINATOR?

AND BEES ARE DISAPPEARING IN LARGE NUMBERS.

BEES ACTUALLY NEED OUR HELP.

MISSING

NAME = Bee
OCCUPATION = POLLINATOR

POSSIBLE REASONS FOR DISAPPEARANCE =

PESTICIDES

PARASITES CALLED VARROA MITES

LACK OF BEE-FRIENDLY FLOWERS

POLLUTION

HONEY

Okay, I take it back, I don't want bees gone. I even sort of want to... help them?

As long as they don't sting me!

PLANTING BEE-FRIENDLY FLOWERS IS A GREAT WAY TO HELP THE BEE POPULATION.

BLUE HYSSOP

CONEFLOWERS

ASTERS

Won't that just attract MORE bees?

HOPEFULLY, YES!

BUT JUST APPROACH A BEE LIKE YOU WOULD A DOG YOU DON'T KNOW.

DON'T GET TOO CLOSE, AND DON'T TRY to TOUCH It.

UNLESS YOU'RE A FLOWER, It SHOULD LOSE INTEREST AND FLY AWAY.

For my parents: my favorite teachers; my biggest cheerleaders.
Thanks for all the unconditional love.
John Thomas Hogan, 1946–2014
Carol Jo Hogan, 1946–2014

Author's very important note: As an illustrator, I've taken some artistic license depicting the bees (mostly honeybees) in this book. Honeybees have 6 legs. Bethany-Barton-book bees appear to have only 2 legs . . . because drawing zillions of bee legs is boring. (Ha! Not really. It just looked messy.) Make sure to check out the endpapers for anatomically correct bees—complete with 6 legs!

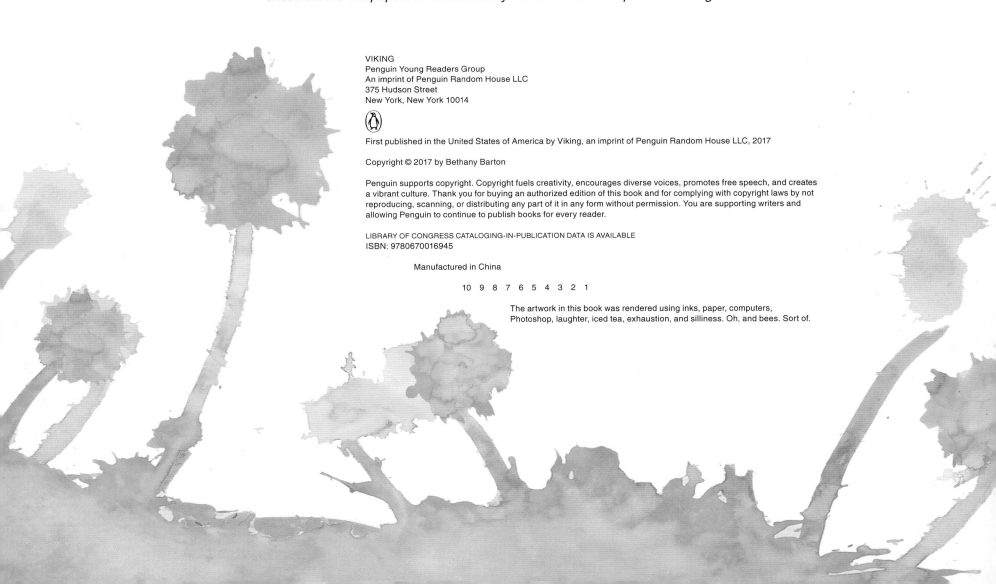

VIKING
Penguin Young Readers Group
An imprint of Penguin Random House LLC
375 Hudson Street
New York, New York 10014

First published in the United States of America by Viking, an imprint of Penguin Random House LLC, 2017

LIBRARY OF CONGRESS CATALOGING-IN-PUBLICATION DATA IS AVAILABLE
ISBN: 9780670016945

Manufactured in China

10 9 8 7 6 5 4 3 2 1

The artwork in this book was rendered using inks, paper, computers, Photoshop, laughter, iced tea, exhaustion, and silliness. Oh, and bees. Sort of.

HORNFACED Bee

(SOLITARY BEE WITH NO QUEEN WHO BUILDS ITS OWN PRIVATE NEST!)

YELLOW-FACED Bee

(INGESTS POLLEN INSTEAD OF COLLECTING IT WITH HAIRS LIKE OTHER BEES!)

CUCKOO Bee

(LAYS EGGS IN THE NESTS OF OTHER BEES, SO ITS LARVAE CAN STEAL THEIR FOOD!)